Could *This* Be What You're Looking For?

Time And Money.com

Create Wealth by Profiting from the Explosive Growth of E-Commerce

Jack Matthews

Time And Money.com

Copyright © 2000 by Jack Matthews
ISBN 0-938716-50-6

Published by
Possibility Press
PossPress@excite.com

Manufactured in the United States of America

Other books by *Possibility Press*:

Brighten Your Day With Self-Esteem
No Excuse!
No Excuse! I'm Doing It
The No Excuse! Workbook
Reject Me—I Love It!
If They Say No, Just Say NEXT!
Are You Living Your Dream?
The Electronic Dream

—Dedication—

This book is dedicated to a new generation of people, who, through e-commerce, are solving their time and money problems — and developing financial freedom.

May this be the key to the door of *your* future — where you *finally* make your dreams come true.

—Acknowledgement—

A special thanks to the entire staff at Possibility Press. They contributed tremendously to making this book what it is.

Your countless hours of dedication will make a positive difference around the world — as millions of people everywhere embrace the golden opportunity of e-commerce.

You're the best!

Jack

— Contents —

*"It is estimated that
50% of all future jobs
will be linked to e-commerce.
And, according to MIT's
Media Lab, e-commerce is
expected to reach
$1 trillion (US) by 2001!
Yes, the Internet is the place
to be if you want
to accelerate your success.
The question is —
'Are you going to take
advantage of it as it begins
to take off?'"*

—Introduction—

Could *This* Be What You're Looking For?

*"The successful person is one
who had the chance and took it"*
–Roger Babson

Yes! E-commerce is really happening. Millions are already buying through the Internet, and people everywhere are starting to do so every day.

Until recently, though, *creating wealth on the Web* has been limited mainly to techno-wizards.

But now, you too, can partake of the enormous profits to be made — *as e-commerce explodes.*

Basically, you could do three things with this new opportunity: 1) Ignore it and hope it goes away; 2) Log on as a consumer, to save time and money; or 3) Log on to profit from its tremendous growth — without affecting your current job or business — as a new e-commerce independent business owner.

Are you going to let this opportunity go — like you may have done with other opportunities in the past? If you ignore this chance, will you regret it later on and say, "If *only* I knew then what I know now"?

What if some people you know run with it, and achieve their dreams and goals? Would you be sorry if you hadn't done so yourself?

Everyone would like to have more time and money! But, when an opportunity comes along to do just that, most people ignore it. They just "settle for" the way things are, and keep doing what they've always done — *hoping* life gets better.

Unfortunately, though, the results are predictable — things usually stay the same or maybe even get worse. But now, here's a chance to change all that.

What two things do most people with time and money freedom have in common? *1) They are ordinary people; and 2) They seized opportunity when it knocked!* They're no smarter or better qualified than you are. They just made the decision and took the appropriate action.

So, where's the new breed of financially free people coming from? And how can *you* become one of them? Read this book. Learn how to solve your time and money problems so you can get out of debt, build wealth — *and live the life you want.*

Have you figured out how you can make money using a computer — *without being a techno-wizard?*

You're about to get a brief overview of the most exciting development the business world has ever known. You'll also learn how *you* can become a part of it — *and make money with it.*

By following a proven pattern of success — coupled with the speed and power of the Internet — you, too, have a new opportunity to prosper.

Remember, only *you* have the final say in what you become, and how you live the rest of your life. Would you like to make a more informed decision about your future? This book could help you.

Can you recall your childhood dreams — where you could be, do, and have *anything* you wanted? How did you imagine your life would be as an adult? If you're not where you'd like to be in life, there could still be time for you to do something about it.

Have you noticed the decline in retail sales at your local malls — *because of e-commerce?*

Do you realize that the US Postal Service and UPS are enjoying significant increases in package deliveries — *because of e-commerce?*

Are you aware that there's a continual decrease in the time people spend watching primetime television — *because more of them are spending an increasing amount of time online?*

Now, you may say, "I don't know how to use a computer," or "I'm not very good at it."

Fortunately, you don't have to be a computer genius to do this business. There are people who can help you. It's a high-tech/high-touch business, where *people* are the most important part. It's people using technology to *leverage* their way to success.

You don't even need to create your own Web site — it's already been done! You simply *use* the site(s) developed and maintained by the supplier(s). The difficult and expensive part is taken care of. You just get online and use them to your advantage.

You're also likely to find your children eager to participate. After all, they've already learned how to use a computer in school. They're familiar with them and think they're fun. In fact, they may even be able to help *you,* if you're not comfortable using a computer!

Opportunity is knocking on the Web — *loud and clear!* Ignore your fears and log on to the Internet …unlock your dreams by browsing the Web site of hope…click on the icon of possibilities…and view your future with anticipation!

Read *Time And Money.com* and learn about the possibilities — *for you!*

— 1 —

E-Commerce Is Exploding! "But How Can *I* Benefit From Its Growth?" You Ask

"...see how you could potentially be a part of this new business revolution — one that holds more promise for more people then anything else ever has before!"

Bill *Gates*, founder of *Microsoft* and the richest man in the world, would not be where he is today if it weren't for computers, the Internet and e-commerce.

Michael Dell, founder of *Dell Computers*, became a multi-millionaire selling computers over the Internet.

Jeff Bezos, founder of *Amazon.com*, became a billionaire selling books via e-commerce.

Steven Jobs and Steve Wozniak, founders of *Apple Computers*, started the personal computer revolution and became "zillionaires."

"That's wonderful for them, but what about *me?"* you ask. Well, here's *your* chance to learn about an exciting independent business opportunity. It uses the technology and ideas they and others developed. And it could take you where you want to go — whether it's to help you realize your wildest dreams, or earn a couple hundred extra dollars a month. It's up to you.

Fortunately, someone thought enough of you to lend you this book. Perhaps they noticed something about you that you may not have seen in yourself.

It could have been something you said. Maybe it was your enthusiasm that caught their attention. Or, perhaps they consider you a friend worthy of sharing good news with.

But, regardless of the reason they lent you this book, you can feel complimented and fortunate that they did.

After you've read this book, you'll probably notice, more than ever, the news stories about the phenomenal growth of e-commerce. You may see figures like the $31 billion in revenue generated last year — with *only* 10% of current computer owners shopping on the Internet!

Do you realize you could save time and money by doing much of your regular shopping on the Internet — *from the comfort of your own home?*

By not having to go from store to store you can avoid crowds, lines, sore feet, and aimless mall searches.

Buying over the Internet thus, saves the average person three hours a week. That adds up to practically an extra day a month to do something else you'd rather do. Wouldn't that be great?

More importantly, you'll begin to see how *you* could potentially be a part of this new business revolution — one that holds more promise for more people than anything else ever has before!

What you won't get though, is something for nothing. This is not a get rich quick scheme. There are no guarantees that this is even what you're looking for.

But — *what if it is?*

This e-commerce based opportunity has been developed to give people, from all walks of life, a chance to *really* succeed.

But, just like any other worthwhile endeavor, it requires effort. And your rewards will be directly related to what you put into it.

Unfortunately, many people are under the illusion that they can keep doing the same things, and somehow their time and money problems will magically resolve themselves. But this is a dangerous belief that typically leads to a lifetime of disappointment and regret.

"You get what you focus on." Did you ever hear that expression? Most people are where they are in life, because *that's* what they've focused on, whether they realize it or not! It simply couldn't be any other way. Now, isn't that true?

Yes, everyone focuses on *something*, and that's what they get. So, to solve your time and money problems and build financial freedom — you need to focus on doing that!

For example, if you focus on watching TV sitcoms, you'll know all about the characters and the stories. But, that's not going to get you financially free. Whereas, if you invest that same time in doing this business, you could solve your time and money problems.

Your dreams and goals are your vision of the future — *that's what successful people focus on.* Pursuing them will give you a sense of satisfaction, and vitality, like nothing else in life can.

You will be pleased and have a great feeling of accomplishment — when you achieve them. And you'll also have a happier, more fulfilling life.

Yes, e-commerce *is* exploding! And fortunately, the steps you need to take to profit from its growth have all been carefully laid out — *paving the way for your success.* All you need to do is ask for help.

— 2 —

Why Might *You* Want to Learn More About This Opportunity?

"It is insane to depend on your employer for security."
— Worth Magazine

W hat's the first thing you need to get different results in your life? You need a *desire* for something you don't already have — a goal or a dream that you really want to come true.

If you're satisfied with your life the way it is, why do anything other than what you're already doing? Why bother, if your life is already exactly the way you dreamed it would be?

Now, you may be saying, "Don't give me that dream stuff." That's okay. But think for a moment — why do *you* do things? Isn't it because you have a desire to get a certain result? That's all we're saying here.

A *dream* or a *goal* is the driving force behind anyone making a positive change — even if it's simply the hope that *next year will be better!*

For example, you probably work a job or have a business to maintain your standard of living — so you can pay your bills and have some of life's little pleasures, right?

The sad reality is, though, that *at least 70% of the population dislikes going to work!* How about you?

Do you go to your job or business only because you believe you *have* to? Or, perhaps you don't know of any other real options?

Maybe you have never even considered the possibilities of using e-commerce to give yourself the results you want. Perhaps you had no idea you could personally make money using the Internet.

What does your financial picture look like? Are you out of debt yet? Are you concerned that you may not have any retirement money left over — after you've put your children through college?

Would you like to take more vacations with your family, have lots of money to spend, and stay as long as you wish? How about retiring early from your job or business?

Are you all stressed out and yet *still* not getting ahead financially—even though you're working overtime, have a second job, or just got promoted?

Are you fed up with your boss? Does it ever seem like your job or business owns *you* rather than you owning *it?*

Do you realize about 500,000 people a year are losing their jobs because of new technology? Are you aware that *entire industries are disappearing* — as new technology replaces the old?

For example, the vinyl record industry is gone — CDs have taken over. Cars use high-tech computerized fuel injection, instead of low-tech mechanical carburetion. Computers have replaced typewriters, and digital TV is replacing dot matrix TV. The world is going increasingly high-tech.

And while the US economy looks strong, it's primarily so because of rapidly increasing consumer debt, which is nearing an astonishing $7 trillion (US)! People are buying more than ever with *borrowed* money on *borrowed* time. In fact, over one million people filed for bankruptcy last year!

Does it seem like your life is being consumed — just trying to pay bills? Do you feel overwhelmed by a growing sense of financial insecurity?

Have you, or has anyone you know of, ever been downsized? Has your company, or others you may have heard of, ever merged or been acquired in a hostile takeover? Has your company, or any you know of, ever relocated or closed facilities — because of cheaper labor abroad? Have you, or has anyone you know of, ever been demoted?

Well, the great news is, you can rise above all of this "garbage" by profiting from the explosive growth of e-commerce. Instead of worrying what might happen, you can be happy being one of the new breed of financially free people who are profiting from the high-tech shift.

Would you like to go fishing, boating, or golfing, or participate in some other sport or hobby you enjoy — *whenever you feel like it?*

Would you find it gratifying to give more generously to your place of worship, and to charities and causes you believe in?

But, no matter what your desires may be— *the key question is simply this...*

How would you like to have all the time and money you need, to do whatever you want to do, whenever you want to do it?

Now, all of this may seem like "pie in the sky" hype, or just plain wishful thinking. Perhaps you feel this way because you may not *personally* know anyone who has *their* time and money problems solved.

If you're like most people, you associate primarily with others at your own socio-economic level. Therefore, you may not have anyone to serve as a role model.

In addition to that, you may not have anyone to help you to move on to your next level of successful living — *except perhaps the person who lent you this book!*

And, when you stop and think about it, most people you know who have the time to do what they want to do, *don't* have the money.

Conversely, most people who have the money *don't* have the time to enjoy it.

Have you ever noticed that?

But, there *are* those who have "set themselves up." They took advantage of a good opportunity when it came along, and developed it to the point where they have achieved financial freedom.

Many financially free people started when they were no better off than the average person, while some were totally broke.

There are people everywhere who are making their dreams come true by operating their own independent e-commerce business.

How would *you* like to join them?

What's *your* biggest dream or goal? Are you now working toward it? Do you want it seriously enough — to put forth some time and effort to accomplish it?

"Don't put all your eggs in one basket." Have you ever heard that sage piece of advice? That's how the wealthy operate. They don't rely on just one source of income.

This business gives you the chance to *diversify* your income by developing — *a strong secondary income.*

Wouldn't it be great to have another source of income equal to or greater than what your current occupation provides? Wouldn't that enable you to dramatically accelerate your wealth. And just think about this — *it just wouldn't matter if you lost or left your job!*

At a minimum, this business can help you save some time and money.

Would you like to open the door to a better life for you and your family? If so — *keep in mind what wealthy people say...*

"Don't just work hard for a living; also work smart for a lifestyle."

Take advantage of the high-tech shift that's occurring throughout the world — *and use the power of the Internet to prosper.*

— 3 —

Shoulda— Coulda— Woulda—

"The follies which a person regrets most in their life are those which they didn't commit to when they had the opportunity."
– Helen Rowland

Recently, there was an article about a man who went to work for *Microsoft* in its early days.

His pay was very low. Even so, he saved up and bought $2,100 worth of stock — because he believed in the company's future. And without buying any additional stock, *he became a multi-millionaire in less than ten years!* Would you have done what he did — if you had been given the same chance?

No one but *you* can decide what you're going to do with *this* opportunity. Like the man who bought the *Microsoft* stock, if you believe enough in the future of e-commerce and take appropriate action, you could profit tremendously in the coming years.

Review the rest of this book with an open, inquisitive mind. Ask the person who shared it with you to show you the Web site.

Then have them introduce you to some of the successful e-commerce independent business owners in your area. This can help you determine the right thing for you to do.

To achieve *different* results in your life, you need to *do something else* that can give you those results.

In fact, many successful people often define insanity as "continuing to do the same things while expecting *different* results"!

Do you know anyone who does that?

What will your life be like in the next two to five years — if you keep doing what you're doing?

How can you tell?

Just look at somebody who's been doing what you do — two to five years longer than you have. That'll probably give you a pretty good idea of where you'll be in life — if you don't do something that can give you what you really want.

And — *remember this...*

If you continue doing what you've always done, you'll just continue to have what you've always had. Nothing is likely to improve, and you probably won't get what you want out of life.

Move ahead while time is still on your side, and e-commerce is starting to boom.

Are you pleased with what you see down the road? If not — *ask yourself these two questions...*

1) If you're not going to take advantage of the explosive growth of e-commerce, then what *will* you do to achieve your dreams and goals?

And...

2) If you don't do it *now*, will you be sorry later?

*"Life moves on, whether we act
as cowards or heroes.
Life has no other
discipline to impose
if we would but realize it,
than to accept life unquestioningly.
Everything we shut our eyes to,
everything we run away from,
everything we deny,
denigrate or despise,
serves to defeat us in the end.
What seems different, scary, or
challenging, can be a source of
beauty, joy, and strength —
when faced with an open mind.
Every moment is a golden one
for those who have the vision
to recognize it as such."*

– Henry Miller

— 4 —

Ch-Ch-Ch-Changes — The Only Thing Constant In Life Is Change

*"Since changes are going on anyway,
the great thing is to learn enough about them so that we
will be able to lay hold of them and turn them in the
direction of our desires. Conditions and events are
neither to be fled from nor passively acquiesced in;
they are to be utilized and directed."*
– John Dewey

When I was a young boy, we would visit my grandparents. One of the things I remember most was mowing the lawn. And since they had a postage stamp-sized yard, they didn't need a power mower.

I'd cut the grass with one of those old-time push mowers — the kind with the long spiral blades that turned with the wheels as you pushed. And even though there was no grass to pick up and bag, my grandmother would give me a dollar when I was done.

Today, things are different. There are options — self-propelled, push power, riding, mulching, and rear-bagging mowers, plus weed wackers, and more.

Yet, even with all the improvements in lawn care technology, one essential ingredient still remains — *someone* has to operate the equipment. These machines and tools simply cannot do the work by themselves. They need the human element — the *high-touch* of people.

People always need to be involved — *or the job will never get done.*

The evolution of the computer has followed much the same trail. From a massive multi-room piece of complicated electronics and machinery, to simple units that can now be held in the palm of your hand. And who knows what's next?

Computers are getting faster and "smarter" with each generation, and can do virtually anything the user might imagine. For example, a computer typed the original manuscript for this book — while I spoke the words! Once again, a person has to add their high-touch to the high-tech, or nothing happens.

It almost sounds like science fiction, doesn't it? Actually, it *was* science fiction at one time! The fact is, new electronic tools and gadgets are being created every day. And they are becoming more available than ever.

In addition to that, these technological marvels are also getting more user-friendly with each new model or program. They are designed to make our lives easier — *by helping us get more done in less time.*

Just as with lawn care equipment, a *person* is needed to control all this high technological power. *Someone* needs to turn the computer on, or it can never even be used — *let alone reach its full potential!*

People are definitely the mainstay of this high-tech business revolution. *Someone* needs to use the tools available in order to benefit from what they can do.

Would you like that someone to be — *you?*

Is there potential for you to solve your time and money problems with this high-tech/high-touch opportunity?

That all depends — *on you.*

The knowledge to help you succeed is readily available through mentors and leaders. Just ask them to show you the way.

But, the *only* way you can build a successful business, of any kind, is to first have a strong enough desire to make some changes in your life — *and then take appropriate action.*

And — *as the saying goes...*

"If you want some things to change in your life, you need to change some things in your life!"

— 5 —

Why Would *You* Want To Embrace The Tremendous Power Of E-Commerce?

"The secret to success in life is for a person to be ready for their opportunity when it comes."
– Benjamin Disraeli

If you're not taking full advantage of e-commerce, you might be making a big mistake! However, by taking full advantage of it, you could gain the competitive edge you need to reach your next level of success.

It is estimated that 50% of all future jobs will be linked to e-commerce. And, according to MIT's Media Lab, e-commerce is expected to reach $1 trillion (US) by 2001! Yes, the Internet is *the* place to be, if you want to accelerate your success.

What you have just read are predictions based on the current trends and the latest technological developments. As great as they are though, none of them can possibly be of any benefit to you without one very important ingredient — *your active participation!*

> The new technology, especially to the nontechnical person, may seem like a miracle. But, it can offer you a promising future — *only* when you seize the opportunity and run with it. Otherwise, it won't do you any good.

No doubt about it — today's communications breakthroughs are making it easier to reach millions of people almost instantly.

But, if you don't let anyone know you're a part of it, all the technology in the world can't help you solve your time and money problems — *or build your financial future.*

To maximize the possibilities you could realize to make your life more like you want it to be, you need to use the tools effectively.

To benefit, you need to *take action* and *share* this powerful e-commerce opportunity.

For example, if Edison hadn't told anyone about the light bulb he had just invented, and instead, kept it to himself, what do you suppose would have become of it? Nothing!

All high-tech developments are worthless — *without the high-touch of people.*

In fact, the *only* way you or anyone else can succeed at anything is to — *take action and share whatever it is you are doing with others.*

If you don't do something to get ahead, you may be left by the roadside as the "success parade" passes you by. Then, 20 years from now, you can say, "I sure wish I had done something with that e-commerce opportunity I looked at, back in the early 2000s!"

Using the appropriate tools is certainly a step in the right direction. And through the process of trial and error, you *might* eventually be able to use them to their fullest potential.

But, what if you could learn what you need to know in a matter of days? Why search for years to find the real capabilities of today's new technology? Well, you *can* speed up the process...

After you read this book, get back with the person who lent it to you. Ask them for more details and what you could do next. Learn as much as you can from someone who's already building an e-commerce business. And, if they're new at it too, don't worry. They can refer you to others with more experience and success.

There are people available who can show you what this high-tech/high-touch business is all about — but it's up to *you* to ask for help.

So, why would you want to embrace the power of e-commerce — and share it with others? *Because it can help you make your dreams come true!*

If you keep it to yourself, it's not going to do you any good. So, start spreading the word.

— 6 —

You May Be Asking, "So, What *Are* The Basic Keys To Success, Anyway?"

"Follow a proven pattern of success — one that has already been developed, and is helping countless others to achieve their dreams and goals."

Everyone in this e-commerce business has the chance to work with people who have become successful independent business owners. And, while everyone has their own business, no one needs to figure everything out for themselves.

So, how *can* you start accelerating the accomplishment of your time and money goals? Simply follow a proven pattern of success — one that has already been developed, and is helping countless others to achieve *their* dreams and goals. That's how people become super successful.

How *can* you better understand how to develop a strong secondary income — with this business? Ask the person you got this book from to show you what you need to do.

So, what *are* the basic keys to success? Simply this — focus on your dreams and goals, grow personally, build mutually beneficial relationships, use the latest high-tech tools, and share this book with others who want to do the same.

And — *this high-tech/high-touch business can help you do that.*

When you grow and invest time in the people around you, and take a genuine interest in their dreams and goals, you can gain a tremendous return.

After all — *no one can be successful alone!*

As an old Chinese proverb says, "If you want a harvest next season, grow a crop. If you want a harvest in ten years, grow a tree. And, if you want a harvest for a lifetime, grow people."

It's only when working in concert with others, who are going in the same direction, that true success can occur.

Just think about all the really successful people you have ever heard of — whether they're an athlete, rock star, movie star, company owner, or other well-known wealthy person.

So — *what do all these people have in common?*

In every single case, you'll find that they have surrounded themselves with other people — employees, teammates, group members, associates, or others — who also want success in that arena.

> The opportunity you are now considering gives you the chance to work with others toward *your* dreams and goals — without a big investment, or any particular talents or gifts. The main thing you need is *desire*.

You can receive all the support you want and need. There are people, informational materials, books, tapes, seminars, and the like, to help you grow to any level of success you may want.

And, while you would be in business *for* yourself, you wouldn't be in business *by* yourself. There are plenty of people around to help you — *as long as you're willing to do your part.*

Remember, all true success is the result of people working together. And that's the cornerstone of what makes this e-commerce business such a solid opportunity.

Outside of this business, most millionaires will not take the time to tell you or show you what they did to become successful — *let alone* help you succeed like they did. Most wealthy people just won't share the secrets of their success. That's unfortunate.

However, in *this* business, you get to associate with wealthy people — most of whom came from the ranks of the average — who can and *will* help you succeed! They've been *there* and have empathy for those who still are.

Unlike many other business opportunities, what you have here is a *system* of success, designed to help those who ask for it. It's people helping people, while using technology to leverage their success. And, as the old saying goes, "Ask and you shall receive."

"So, why in the world would someone, who's already wealthy and successful, want to help *me?*" you may ask. Now let's just think about that for a minute. For example, why would a movie star keep on acting? Why would someone who's made millions keep on going?

Why do they keep going — *even though they "have it made"?*

It could be for any number of reasons: They love what they do; they enjoy associating with and helping others in their field; they go on to support charities and establish foundations; they use their excess wealth to make investments, and set up or purchase other businesses; or they do whatever else they choose — *because they have the time and money to do so.*

And it's heart warming when you discover, that's also how people are in this business. If you doubt it, ask the person who lent you this book to meet some of them — *then decide for yourself.*

— 7—

Time And Money And The *Real* "Secret" Of The Wealthy

"...as the old expression goes, 'Time is money.' But, as you share this business with others, that adage begins changing to — 'Time earns money.'"

When asked what their main concerns in life are, most people say time and money — the *lack* of time and money! There always seems to be too much month left at the end of the money. As a result, people often work extra hours or a second job, in an attempt to make up for it.

When *that* doesn't work, they may go into or get deeper in debt — making their financial situation even worse. And, as soon as they begin catching up on their bills, they may realize they've created *yet another* undesirable situation. There's little or no *time* to spend with the most important people in their lives — or to do the things they'd really love to do.

While the bills may get paid, their quality of life suffers, as does that of their families, who rarely see them. And everybody seems all stressed out, and generally not very happy. They feel like they're on a treadmill, running "a million miles an hour," but getting nowhere fast. Have *you* ever had that experience?

> Becoming an independent business owner can change all of that. By having your own e-commerce business, and *buying* various consumer products and other goods and services via the Internet, the very first thing you'll *save* is *time*. As mentioned previously, the time you spent going to the store, to get many of those items, is now yours to do something else with!

The first thing you'll *earn* when *building* this e-commerce business is *also* time — more specifically, *your* time. And, as the old expression goes, "Time is money." But as you share this business with others, that adage begins changing to — "Time *earns* money."

Those who understand the true potential of e-commerce may join you. And, as you'll learn, you'll also make *money* based on what *they* spend!

Continue repeating that process, and you could develop the best form of income there is — *ongoing residual income.* This is the *real* "secret" of the wealthy — having money come in even when you're *not* working — instead of trading time for dollars, like you do when you work a job.

Share this business with enough people, who also take advantage of it, and your income from it can become residual. You wouldn't be subject to demotions, layoffs, downsizing, or forced retirements. It's a wonderful example of what some time and effort invested *now* can do for your future.

When your income from this business gets big enough, you'll no longer be concerned about the pitfalls of working at a job or another business. And you can continue receiving this income, *regardless of what you do,* as long as your business is solid. In fact, it could even grow — *whether or not you're still building it!* Wouldn't that be great?

Most importantly, you owe it to yourself and your family to see just what residual income is all about — and what it can do for you and your lifestyle. You can learn more about the details from the person you borrowed this book from. And you may be surprised by what you discover!

> As others see you becoming happier and more successful, *they* may approach *you* to find out what you're doing. When they do, simply lend them this book and show them the Web site — then let these tools do their jobs — *for you!*

> If they're *still* not sure, you might suggest they *try* the business out before making any decisions. Lend them some of these books and suggest that they simply share them with a few friends and acquaintances.

What could result is a chance for you, and the person helping you, to get together with those people. They can then learn more about the opportunity and the potential — *all at the same time!*

If, after that, some say they have no further interest, that's okay. You haven't lost anything — *they* did! Just keep going.

You're bound to find some folks who don't want to miss out on this opportunity, and will use it to — *make their dreams come true.*

There are people everywhere who want to take advantage of the explosive growth of e-commerce.

You can count on it.

There are people everywhere who would like to have more time and money, and ongoing residual income — the *real* "secret" of the wealthy!

You can be sure of that.

— 8 —

Share This Opportunity With Others, And *Leverage* Your Way To Financial Freedom

"...word-of-mouth (sharing) accelerates online to an almost unfathomable degree...with the click of a mouse, now people can tell thousands...our business recognizes the shift of power toward the (people)."
– Jeff Bezos, Founder and CEO, Amazon.com

Did you ever see a really good movie, and then recommend it to others? That's great — but *you* didn't make any money for doing that, *did you?* You helped the movie producers, actors, and theater owners get rich. But *you* didn't make a dime!

Now, how would you like to *start making money* from your recommendations? Simply start sharing this book with others — *and you can accomplish two things...*

First, you'll find the people who are looking for an opportunity to make money with a computer. Second, you'll also be showing *them* exactly what *they* need to do to begin building *their* own independent e-commerce business.

When that happens — *you* can begin getting paid because *you* were the one who recommended the opportunity to *them!*

It's simple — *just share this book with others!* They can then duplicate your example with the people *they* come in contact with.

The big benefit is that you, and those who associate with you, can use the power of this book and the Internet — to work for both *you* and *them!* It's a real win-win situation, and an efficient use of tools.

> You'll also save time — which is probably the first thing you may want more of in your busy life. Making more money is certainly a wonderful, marvelous thing. But what good does it do you — *unless you have the time to enjoy it?*

This book simply introduces people to this e-commerce business, covers some of the basics, and answers a few common questions. If they want more information, show them the Web site. Those who understand the real potential of doing business on the Internet, and want to take advantage of the opportunity, will call *you!*

You come back into the picture *only* after they express interest or want to learn more. If they don't — *you just move on!*

You're looking for people who really want to make some dreams come true, or perhaps just want to save some time and money by purchasing via the Internet. This book and today's technology gives you the power to find those people — *more people than you could probably ever imagine!*

For those who want to maintain the status quo, that's fine. It's their choice. As the old saying goes, "You can lead a horse to water, but you can't make him drink." He's got to be thirsty! And you're simply looking for some "thirsty" people.

Sharing this book with others will save you time *and* money. It eliminates the extra work you would otherwise have to do with people who may not be interested anyway.

Not spending any time on someone who would say no, is a great advantage. It's one of the most positive things that can happen when building any business — *you're not wasting your precious time.*

Now understand, there are three possible outcomes from sharing this book and the opportunity it presents: 1) They won't be interested in anything offered here; 2) They would like to save time and money by purchasing items via the Internet; or 3) They are also interested in becoming an e-commerce independent business owner — to create a strong secondary income, or perhaps earn a couple hundred extra dollars a month.

And remember, just because someone doesn't want to save time and money, or move on when *you* do, doesn't mean they won't want to later on. Then, too, some people may be jealous of you, criticize you, and even try to hold you back! "Misery loves company."

But, deep down inside, they'll probably respect you. Furthermore, their attitude or circumstances, could change at any time — and they just might call *you!* No matter what, the more people you share this opportunity with, without getting hung up on any individual response, the faster your business can grow — *and the more success you can achieve.*

Now, ask yourself — "How many happy people do I know?" If you're like most, probably very few.

There are people everywhere going to bed every night, hoping and praying for an opportunity like this to come along. They're sad and maybe even depressed — *and you can help them!*

Sharing this business could be one of the nicest things you do for someone. And, as in sharing or giving anything to anybody, or in doing a good deed, you simply need to feel good about it.

How anybody responds to your gesture is no reflection on you — it just depends on *them*. It depends on how they feel about themselves, on where they're at in life, what they're doing now, and where they want to go.

Share this business because you believe it can help others — regardless of what you think they might say or do about it. It simply doesn't matter what they think, say, or do. Some people will be grateful, while others may simply be afraid to admit they could use some help. That's just human nature.

The point is, don't be concerned about how any particular person responds. All that matters is what *you* say and do for yourself. It's what *you* believe this e-commerce business can do for you and your family that counts the most.

There are millions of people who *are* interested in saving and earning time and money — and *are* ready to move on. There are millions of people who *are* looking for the right opportunity — *and you could be the one to share it with them.*

Since *time is money* and *time earns money*, as described earlier, you need to invest some time now to get more back later — with "interest." It's a basic law of success. And, while we all have only 24 hours a day, when you share this opportunity with enough people, who in turn do the same thing, you begin multiplying what you can accomplish.

This business can work for you, somewhat like a corporation that becomes more profitable as it grows. More employees benefit the corporation by increasing productivity, leading to higher profits.

But, *unlike* a corporation, you don't have any employees or their associated problems — *because everyone is in their own business!*

As J. Paul Getty, the world's richest man when he was alive, once said, "I'd rather have 1% of the results of 100 men's efforts than 100% of the results of just my own efforts."

This business enables you to *leverage* your time and multiply your results — by sharing and associating with other people — *without having to hire them!*

Share this opportunity with others, and leverage your way to financial freedom.

It's only when you work in association with other people that you can become truly successful. Working in concert with others forms the basis for creating a solid business capable of generating ongoing residual income.

This is the *key* to solving your time and money problems — *and becoming financially free.*

— 9 —

So, Why Is *Movement* More Important Than Motivation?

"Regardless of where you are now in your life, if it's not where you want to be, there is only one solution — you need to do something different!"

Now that you have read this far, you probably have an exciting sense of what's possible for you with e-commerce. And, apparently, the person you received this book from saw something in you that told them you could do this — *if you choose to.*

Have you begun dreaming about your future? This is certainly an important first step. Are you motivated by what you have learned so far, and believe that what you envision for yourself *is* achievable?

> That's great if that's how you feel. But you need to be honest with yourself — *that's not enough!* You can feel motivated all you want and accomplish nothing more than having grand wishes. Or, you can see this as your real chance to create the life you want and — *actually do something about it.*

Whether you totally understand this business or not, is less important than working with what you *do* understand. You can learn more about it as you go along.

For example, like starting a new job, getting married, or becoming new parents, you begin these activities without knowing much about them. You just learn as you go. Nobody waits to know everything about something new before they begin doing it!

Your enthusiasm, and actually sharing this business with others, is much more important than knowing all the details. You're *going* somewhere — *and that's what causes people to want to associate with you.*

And when the people you're sharing this opportunity with see that it can help *them*, they'll be more inclined to be interested. After all — *nobody wants to miss out on a good thing.*

Perhaps that's why *you* may want to get back to the person you got this book from.

The technology you have access to is the latest available. And the success system that can help you achieve what *you* want is the foundation for this business. It helps independent business owners make their dreams come true.

That system, along with the power of the Internet, gives you tremendous potential.

And since this business is people-oriented, you never have to let the technology intimidate you. It's simply a great new tool to help you succeed.

However — *sharing the opportunity with other people is the main key to your success!*

This book enables you to easily get started in this business. All you need to do is finish reading it, and contact the person who shared it with you.

If you have no interest, simply give this book back to that person. Or else, hand it to someone you may know or meet who *is* looking for an opportunity to make their life better.

However, if you think there might be something in this for you and your family, ask for more information. And be sure to ask the person who gave you this book what to do next.

Regardless of where you are now in your life, if you're not where you want to be, there is only one solution — *you need to do something different!*

If you want to be successful with this business, just begin sharing it with other people. After all, surveys show that 95% of all people would like to have a business of their own. They just need somebody to show them the way.

And that someone could be — *you!*

So, why is *movement* more important than motivation?

It's simply what you *do* that counts!

— 10—

Get Good Advice And … Watch Out For Excuses!

"Do yourself a favor — be skeptical. Examine this opportunity closely. Get all the facts — the real facts — from people who know this business. Never rely on opinions, hearsay, innuendo, or excuses — and don't let anyone steal your dream."

We benefit most by observing and learning from those who are more successful than we are. If you can meet someone who is successful in this business, wouldn't it make sense to ask *them* how they did it *— and how you can, too?*

Remember the expression, "Give a man a fish, and he can eat for a day. But, show him how to fish, and he can eat for a lifetime"? Wouldn't it be great to "fish" better than you already do, by learning from somebody who knows how?

Now, who is likely to give you the best advice — someone who's actually *successful* in this business, or someone who just has an opinion about it?

Most people prefer learning from an experienced person. But what some of them turn around and do is completely the opposite!

What is baffling, is that there are people who will look at an opportunity and then "consult" with a friend. Now mind you, their friend may have no experience in any kind of business — let alone something as cutting edge as this. Amazingly, some people will *still* follow their "advice"!

For example, if you want financial advice, wouldn't it make sense to go to a financial consultant? You wouldn't even think of going to someone who just filed for bankruptcy now, would you?

Do yourself a favor — *be skeptical.* Examine this opportunity closely. Get all the facts — *the real facts* — from people who *know* this business.

Have the person who lent you this book bring you to a get together or seminar.

Get introduced to a variety of people from all walks of life. While many are probably just starting out — some have already achieved various levels of success.

Ask them why they got into the business, how they feel about the potential of e-commerce, and how they became successful.

Get facts — *not opinions, hearsay, innuendo, or excuses* — and don't let *anyone* steal your dream.

There are people who, deep down inside, would like more success. But, unfortunately, they sabotage it by making excuses — usually without even realizing it. It's just a habit.

They tell themselves they don't want to learn how to "fish" any better — because they may fear change. It's sad, but that's what keeps them from getting what they really, really want.

Such people often complain but never *do* anything about it. They may say, "We're doing okay." But what does *that* mean? Are they *really* satisfied with their life?

Or they might say, "Money isn't everything."

And while this is certainly true, it may not seem so for those who *lack* the money they need — because they're always running out of it. The end of every month seems to be financially stressful.

Some people may even go so far as to say, "I'm not materialistic" — *when they simply can't afford something.* That's understandable. But the fact is, the more someone can afford to buy, the less importance they place on material things!

And, as *Jeff Bezos* of *Amazon.com* explained in an interview with *Yahoo! Internet Life* magazine, "Once you get to a certain lifestyle, money doesn't really matter very much. Below that point, it matters tremendously."

For example, if someone's car breaks down and they don't have the money to fix it, that situation could lead to an argument. Whereas, if they've got the money, it's easy to get the car repaired.

And while money doesn't buy happiness, it certainly gives you options. Besides which, it also helps you eliminate financial stress.

Some people criticize those with a lot of money, for whatever reason.

But money is the *only* thing that can do what it does. It gives us a home, feeds us, clothes us, builds our churches and hospitals, and enables us to pay for our children's college educations. It also provides us with transportation, buys some of life's little pleasures, and enables us to go on vacation. And besides all of that, money gives us the ability to donate to the charities of our choice.

Money isn't a luxury — *it's a necessity.* Without it, there's not much you can do. The poor can't help the poor. However, with excess money, you can do *more* for yourself, as well as help those less fortunate.

And some people may even say that, "Money is the root of all evil."

But the truth is, money is just ink on paper — a medium of exchange for goods provided or services rendered. Money is neutral. And in the hands of good people, a lot of good can be done with it.

To make more money then, you simply need to render more services or provide more goods. And this business gives you an opportunity to do that, and more.

Then there are those who say, "I don't have time."

But the fact is, *everyone* has 24 hours a day. Your success, or lack of it, depends on how you use *your* 24 hours. The advantages of this business are useless to you, unless you do something productive with it during those 24 hours.

Remember, *time is your greatest asset.* Invest it wisely!

And finally, there are some people who honestly believe they'll do something in the future to change their lot in life. They may say things like, "I'll get around to it someday," or perhaps a simple, "Someday I'll...."

These folks would like their lives to be better, and realize they need to do something to make it so. But, they put off taking any action — waiting for circumstances to improve.

Sadly for them though, nothing gets better. And *someday* typically turns into a new word called *never*. Until they make a decision to do something with this business, their procrastination keeps them stuck in "never-never" land.

Those who truly succeed in life don't let circumstances get in their way. They realize that there's always *something* going on in their lives, and that there's no "perfect" time to do anything. They use their circumstances as a *reason* to move on, instead of an excuse to stay where they are. That's how they became successful.

To move ahead in life, don't let anything or anyone stop you. After all, you're the one who has to live your life. No one can do it for you. Why not make it the way you want it?

As the saying goes, "He who hesitates is lost." Get out from under the circumstances and start dreaming of how your life can be. Turn any excuses you may have into reasons. Let your dreams for a better life drive you forward — *now!*

Remember to get advice from people who know this business, and watch out for excuses. Then decide what is right for you. Just be honest with yourself. Don't cheat yourself out of the future you would sincerely like to have.

— 11 —

What Are The Main Ingredients & Advantages Of An *Ideal* Business?

"Aspiring millionaires are best advised not to go to work for big corporations. In fact, 85% of America's millionaires own their own business...."
– US News & World Report

Most wealthy people own a business. If you have a job, you only get paid at a wholesale rate — your employer has to make a profit on what you do. But, when you own a business — *you keep the profits!*

"So, what *are* some of the advantages and ingredients of an *ideal* business?" you may ask.

First of all, you need to be able to work your current occupation while you build your business.

"Don't quit your day job," is sound advice for a very good reason. Don't do anything where you could put yourself and your family in a financially risky, stressful situation — where you can't even meet your daily needs.

Next, an ideal business is *home-based* so you have low overhead, with no additional rent or mortgage, and low start-up costs. You can run it from the comfort of your own home or apartment — *with little or no risk.*

You would also have no employees to hire and support, nor would you have to deal with the other challenges they would bring. Instead, you could work with your family and friends — if you want to.

You would have *no boss* — no one to answer to except yourself — and no set hours.

The income potential would be great, and the prospects for expansion would be virtually limitless, with no territorial boundaries. And you could build it anywhere your supplier(s) operate.

Your business would be "portable" — you could run it wherever you have access to a computer (except at your job, of course!). You could use a laptop computer, or even visit your local public library, and use their equipment — if you don't have a computer of your own.

You would be able to buy quality consumer goods and services that are in demand, and at a discount. You would also have a money-back guarantee and receive excellent service.

Many of the products would be consumable — leading to continuous consumption — *enabling you to earn ongoing residual income!*

Your business would be willable to your heirs, as well as offer you certain tax advantages. The tax laws, at least in the US, favor those in business. There are things you would buy *anyway* that you can use as deductions.

For example, you could buy a company car with pre-tax dollars. You could also write off the portion of your home that you use totally for your business.

You would have a great compensation plan and receive your income checks on time. Your supplier(s) would operate with integrity, and have an outstanding reputation in the marketplace.

Your supplier(s) would offer a main Web site, which would keep track of and ideally give you access to your business growth, structure, and volume. You would also have the ability to make purchases online and conduct e-commerce.

In addition to that, the Web site would enable you to connect with the people you are associated with. It would serve as a communications tool to keep everyone informed and up to date.

You would be given the opportunity to associate with upbeat, positive people — *some of whom could mentor and lead you to success.* You would be in an environment where you'd be able to build the relationships that are key to building your business.

Regardless of how great the Internet is, you still can't build wealth with e-commerce just sitting in front of the computer. As with any business, *people* are the most important ingredient for your success. And an *ideal* business combines high-touch with high-tech — *the best of both worlds.*

Training sessions, seminars and conventions would be available to facilitate your learning and motivation. You would also have access to books, tapes, videos, and perhaps CD-ROMs, as well as other materials for your personal growth and business development. You wouldn't have to figure everything out for yourself.

As an independent business owner, you would have a unique opportunity to participate in e-commerce — *with all the advantages of an ideal business.*

The person who lent you this book can give you more information, or refer you to another e-commerce business owner who can help you.

— 12 —

Does This Business Really Work?

"In five years, all companies will be Internet companies, or they won't be companies at all."
– Andy Grove, Chairman, Intel

No! Not by itself. The truth is, *nothing* works by itself— not even the Internet. And this business doesn't work by itself either. *People* make it work.

This business is just an opportunity that people use as a *vehicle* to get the results they want in their lives. And the results *you* get depend strictly on your *desire* and the *effort* you put into it.

The irony of it all is that it could still be done without the advances in technology. You could still achieve wealth and independence using the tried and true principles of success — without ever using a computer. Countless people have already done so, before the age of e-commerce. But now, with the Internet, technology is becoming more and more essential for you to achieve success.

> So today, many more people can achieve the level of freedom they want with less time and effort. They are able to accelerate their success *because* they're using the latest technological tools available.

In addition to technology, they also use the more traditional "tools" for personal and business development that have worked for years.

For instance, they read positive books to develop themselves personally. They also listen to motivational and educational tapes of successful people, who came from various backgrounds.

Besides that, they attend training sessions, seminars and conventions to learn more and stay motivated. There they meet others who are at the same point in their journey of success — as well as those who are where they want to be — and every level in between.

Success isn't attained simply by scrapping the old and replacing it with the new. Things aren't changed merely for the sake of change. It's keeping the things that work, like the tools used for personal and business development, and incorporating the new technology to suit the needs of the times — *and the people using it.*

The way to achieve the greatest, fastest success you possibly can is by adding high-tech tools to the high-touch foundation that successful businesses have used for years.

The fact that this business uses high technology may be what attracted you. Perhaps, you were never interested in any kind of opportunity before. But, since this business is *Internet*-based, you may be seriously looking at it.

Because of the high-tech shift occurring in the world today, there are more people everywhere who will take advantage of this opportunity. You may not realize it, but you probably know some of them.

Up to this point, you've learned why this could be a great opportunity for you. You've also learned why it's so exciting, and discovered a little of what it's all about. But, as you know, unless *you* take what you've learned and *do* something with it, these are only words in a book.

As you may recall from what was said earlier, you can simply *try* this business — *before* you actually do it. Doesn't that make you feel more comfortable? After all, there just aren't many opportunities you can *try* before you make a decision to participate!

In other words — *there's no risk on your part.*

So, what would it take for you to prove to yourself that you can make this work for you? How many people would you be willing to share it with before you say *yes* to your future? More importantly, are you willing to take a chance to find out?

> Finish this book and ask for more details. Then simply pass it along to someone else — *and watch what happens!* Share this book and the opportunity it presents with as many people as you can. See for yourself that you can do it.

What could possibly happen if a couple of the people you lend this book to say yes, after seeing the Web site? What if they also go on to build a huge business?

Know the answer?

You could start receiving ongoing residual income — on the success *they've* built. That's just the way it works!

It's similar to someone getting a royalty on a CD they've recorded, or on something they've invented — *only you don't have to be gifted or talented!*

Once again, all you need to do to get started is to have a desire for something more in your life — *and share this book with others.*

It's as simple as that.

— 13 —

So, What's The "Secret" To Success Beyond Your *Wildest* Dreams?

"It may come as a surprise to you, but most people don't solve their time and money problems and become wealthy, because they are gifted or talented! They simply have a strong desire to do so and take action to reach their goals, and then — they become wealthy in the process."

What if participating in e-commerce could help you achieve the life you've always wanted?

Imagine what your world would be like when you've succeeded beyond your *wildest* dreams.

Where would you be living? What would you be doing? Who would you be spending more time with? What would you own?

There is one common ingredient that everyone possesses — *those who enjoy a high level of success, that is...*

> They've all discovered and fostered this key ingredient to be where they are today. They live wherever they want, spend time with whomever they choose, and do the things they've always wanted to do...and more!

They also have no worries about finances, and can easily meet their monthly payments — because there just aren't any! And they can send their children to the schools of their choice.

The "secret" to living successfully, beyond your wildest dreams, is really quite simple.

Yet many people find themselves on such a treadmill in their everyday "life," that they never discover the secret. They are so caught up in the "rat race," rushing from home to work and back again, that they never even stop to think about it.

Some might call this activity — *a "rut."*

But *now,* you're about to learn that secret. Some of you may cast it off as too simple, while others may shake your heads in disbelief. Yet, there will be those of you who will agree. You will begin to understand that what you're being introduced to is a *vehicle* you can use to get you where you really want to go.

So — *believe it or not...*

The secret to success beyond your wildest dreams is to first — *have wild dreams!*

Now, before you may call this nonsense, continue reading a few more paragraphs to learn why this is true.

Like most people, you probably haven't had a massive fortune fall into your lap. Whatever you've accomplished in life so far, you've probably had to work hard for.

But — *you need to ask yourself one key question...*

Have you been working *towards something*, or simply working to "keep your head above water," as the old saying goes?

Has your life become a tiring, boring grind — *day in and day out?* Are you tired of just paying bills and not getting what you want out of life?

What keeps you going? Isn't it simply the thread of hope that *someday* your life will be better? And has it ever been a desire of yours just to have more peace of mind about things?

The trouble is, by now you have probably found that your occupation simply *won't* enable you to live the life you really want.

And you probably won't win the lottery, either, or inherit a large sum of money.

The point is, very few people become wealthy without being in a *vehicle* that can enable them to attain it.

Becoming an e-commerce independent business owner *can* help you achieve your dreams and goals — provided you have a desire for a better life —by taking advantage of this opportunity.

With your *wildest* dreams solidly before you, you can continue until you realize them. Setbacks and obstacles may slow you down — *but you won't let them stop you.*

When you know where you're going, you're more inclined to keep going. Focus on what you really want, and continue doing what you need to do, to accomplish your goal. You'll then create the momentum you need to succeed.

Your wildest dreams will drive you to take the next step, and then the next. And before too long, you'll find yourself getting closer and closer to making your dreams come true. You'll find yourself getting closer to living the life you really want.

When you get back with the person who shared this book with you, you can learn how to make this opportunity work for you.

And while learning how is important, knowing *why* you need to do it is the *only* reason you'll ever do anything. As long as you know why you want your wildest dreams to come true, that's all you need to begin your quest. Your *why* is the main driving force behind making your wildest dreams come true.

Don't you agree?

It may come as a surprise to you, but most people don't solve their time and money problems and become wealthy because they are gifted or talented!

They do so because they have a strong desire and take action to reach their goals — *and then, they become wealthy in the process!*

They simply apply themselves in a vehicle, like this e-commerce business, that can give them the results they're looking for.

What *do* you want out of life, anyway? Have you seriously thought about that lately? Are you tired of "the rat race" you may be in — in a hurry — but not getting where you want to go?

1) So what *are* your wildest dreams? Take out a piece of paper and write them down now.

2) Would you really like to see them come true?

3) Do you respect yourself enough, to do what it takes to give yourself the life you want?

4) Isn't it time for you to make a move — and *do something* that is capable of giving you the results you so earnestly want and deserve?

*"Those who have
attained things worth
having in this world have
worked while others
idled, have persevered when
others gave up in despair,
have practiced early
in life the valuable habits
of self-denial, industry,
and singleness of
purpose. As a result, they
enjoy the success so
often erroneously attributed
to good luck."*

– Grenvill Kleisen

— 14 —

No, No,
A Thousand Times
No!

*"To help yourself move on,
you may need to pay attention to someone
who kept taking just one more chance
to see his dream come true. You may just learn something
— from someone who absolutely refused to quit."*

He was turned down over 1,000 times by some of the best restaurant people in the world — before he even *started* to succeed. So, you might be asking, "What could I possibly learn from someone who's been rejected over 1,000 times?"

Nothing, if you don't want to! But you might want to take a lesson from someone who — after more than 1,000 noes — was not willing to let those rejections steal his dream or determine his destiny.

To help yourself move on, you may need to pay attention to someone who kept taking just *one more chance* to see his dream come true.

You just might learn something from someone who absolutely refused to quit, until he got a *yes* — which occurred after 1,009 noes. And he was 66-years-old when he started!

Colonel Sanders, of *Kentucky Fried Chicken* fame, was one of those people who just kept on going — in *spite* of all the challenges. And by doing so, he started one of the most successful fast food restaurant chains in the world.

> There are probably others, closer to you, who have lived through many rejections — yet they *still* continue to follow their dreams. And these people *could* help you achieve yours as well. So, *who* are they?

One of them could be — *the person who lent you this book!*

They believe you *may* have the potential, and *hopefully,* a sincere desire to be more successful. And, like Colonel Sanders, they keep on going until they create the life they want. They don't let anyone or anything stand in their way.

They're just doing whatever it takes — *to get the results they want.*

How about — *you?*

When you get back with them, share some of your wildest dreams and goals. They, or an associate of theirs, can help you put together an action plan. They can help get you on the path to solving your time and money problems, achieving your dreams and goals — *and attaining financial freedom.*

As mentioned earlier, it's okay to be skeptical about something new. In fact, it's strongly recommended. Let that healthy caution make you look *really hard* at the opportunity you are considering here.

When you see the potential this e-commerce business represents for you, you just might fall in love with your wildest dreams. Congratulations!

Go ahead and do it — because you *now* have a real opportunity, and a vehicle with which you can make them come true.

Go ahead and do it — *and become a successful independent business owner.* Other people have done it to make *their* wildest dreams come true, and *you* can do it, too.

"Opportunity can benefit no one who has not fitted themselves to seize it and use it. Opportunity woos the worthy, but shuns the unworthy. Prepare yourself to grasp opportunity and opportunity is likely to come your way. It is not so fickle, capricious and unreasoning as some say."

– B.C. Forbes

—15—

If *Only* I Had Taken The Chance… When It Came Along

"If your life is ever going to get better, you'll have to take a chance. There is simply no way you can grow — without taking chances."
– David Viscot

As they say, hindsight is always 20/20. At the beginning of this book, you read about a man who went to work for *Microsoft*, bought some stock and became a millionaire. He couldn't possibly have known that would've happened to him! He just believed in the company — *and the opportunity for himself to create wealth with it.*

Would you have bought some *Microsoft* stock as well — *back in the early days?*

Another gentleman, from Maryland, had some money to invest. He found a small bank that was selling shares for only a dollar each. He bought 25,000. In a few years, that same bank was taken over at a price of almost $22 a share. On a $25,000 investment, he received over $550,000!

Where could *you* get that kind of "inside" information? More importantly, what if you were able to gain some insight concerning the future and the possibilities for you with this business? Would you *do* anything about it?

We've all heard stories like these before. In fact, you may have already passed on some other opportunities, prior to this e-commerce business — which you are now considering.

For example, *Wal-Mart, McDonalds* and others have made rich people out of many early believers. At that time, most had only a hunch and some faith — that they would do well with these companies.

But it wasn't the information they were given that made them wealthy...

It was what they *did* with that information that made the difference in their lives. It was *the chance they took* that helped them realize their dreams.

So now, what are *you* going to do with the information you've just learned? Are you going to use it to make a difference in your life?

Are you going to take this chance to grow and make your dreams come true — like the people you've just read about?

Armed with the "20/20" foresight you've just developed, will you use it to your advantage?

You now have the "inside" information that can help you solve your time and money problems — *and achieve financial freedom.* What you do with it is up to you.

The big questions are...
"What are you
going to do
about securing
your financial future,
now that you've
been given the chance?
Will you pass on solving your
time and money problems?
Or...will you take action,
do something
to improve your life...
and make your
dreams come true?"

— 16 —

Isn't It About Time For Your Life To Improve? This Just *Might* Be *Your* Chance…

"You're the only one who can decide how much you want your dreams to come true. And you're the only one who can take the action necessary to make it happen — for you and your family."

You are now at a crossroad. You now have some information about an exciting cutting edge business opportunity that could have a tremendous impact on your future.

Fortunately, more information is available. In fact, everything you may want to know is available. You can get it from the person you got this book from — or through other successful independent business owners.

The point is — *you can get whatever you need to make an informed decision.*

However, without a decision to take action, all you have here is some information. If you do nothing with it, you will gain nothing from it. And, as with any other opportunity, there are no guarantees.

But — *if you keep doing what you're now doing, where will you be in the next two to five years?*

Will you be living the life you want — or will you just keep on doing the same old thing? Will you have the time and money you need to secure your future, or will you be living paycheck to paycheck?

According to a recent study by a large insurance company, *95%* of most people's disposable income is used to take care of debts! That sure doesn't leave much to build a secure future with — now does it?

If you have the desire to move on in life, get back with the person who shared this book with you. Meet some people in the business, check out the Web site — *and get started.*

Imagine the possibilities for yourself and your family. This just *might* be the opportunity you've been looking for — the one that can take you to where want to go.

So — *what other opportunities do you have?*

Will you forego yet *another* chance, and let *this* opportunity slip through your fingers? Will you be like the millions of folks who *didn't* invest in *Microsoft,* and *didn't* become millionaires?

Or, will you take some action *now* and take control of your destiny? Will you act *now* and accelerate your success? *Remember...*

You're the *only* one who can decide how much you want your dreams to come true. And you're the *only* one who can take the action necessary to make it happen — for you and your family.

So — *what are you going to do?*

You could now be holding the key to the opportunity of a lifetime — right in the palm of your hand. But, what are you going to *do* about it?

You may want to read this book again and think — *really stop and think* — about your life so far and how you feel about it.

Are you happy with where you are? Would you like to accomplish more? Would you like to do some of the things you've always dreamed of — but didn't quite have the time or money to do?

Granted, nothing is for everybody. But, can you imagine this opportunity helping you make your dreams come true? *Wouldn't that be great?*

Just think of all the successful, wealthy people you know of. They're living *their* dreams. And, if *they* can do it, so can *you*. In fact, they once might have been in a situation like yours — or maybe even worse.

The basic difference is, they applied themselves to something that was *capable* of rewarding them appropriately for their efforts. *That's simply what successful people do.*

If they're doing something that's *not* producing the results they want, they do something else that *can*. It's that simple, and it's just a choice!

Now you may ask, "What are the odds I can make it in this business?"

But — *the real question is...*

What are the odds you'll make it if you *don't* do this business?

So — are you *finally* going to go for your dreams? Are you *finally* going to go for the life you really, really want?

Are you sick and tired of being sick and tired, and ready to say — *"Enough already. Now it's **my** turn"?*

As suggested earlier, honestly answer these two simple questions...

1) <u>If you're not going to take advantage of the explosive growth of e-commerce, then what will you do to achieve your dreams and goals?</u>

And...

2) <u>If you don't do it now, will you be sorry later?</u>

*   *   *

To learn more about how you can use the power of e-commerce to solve your time and money problems, and build wealth, contact the person who lent you this book:

Name_____

Phone (____)_____**e-mail** _____

Street_____

City_____**State**____**Zip**_____

*   *   *

Now Go Share This Book With Others

*   *   *

"Do yourself a favor
— be skeptical.
Examine this opportunity
closely.
Get all the facts
— the real facts —
from people who know
this business.
Never rely on opinions,
hearsay, innuendo,
or excuses — and
don't let anyone steal
your dream."

Tomorrow
is the first day
of the rest
of your life.
Use it
to start
making your
dreams come
true....